Regulating Artificial Intelligence

How Governments Control AI Systems

By Joe Correa

Published by Live Stronger Faster

First Edition

Table of Contents

Overview 5

Chapter 1: Why Governments Regulate AI....11

Chapter 2: The EU AI Act.... 17

Chapter 3: U.S. AI Policy in Effect.... 22

Chapter 4: China's AI Rules & What You Should Know About Them.... 27

Chapter 5: Military AI & It's Potential Power....32

Chapter 6: Surveillance AI Used By The Government.... 38

Chapter 7: Risk-Based Regulation in Modern Life....43

Chapter 8: Corporate Compliance Around the World.... 48

Chapter 9: Penalties & Fines in the World of AI.... 53

Chapter 10: The Future of AI Law & What It Means to You.. 58

Chapter 11: The Global AI Order....63

Chapter 12: Humanity in the Age of Regulated Intelligence.. 67

Final Thoughts.... 72

Overview

Artificial intelligence is no longer a laboratory experiment, a startup curiosity, or a futuristic concept waiting to arrive. It now decides who gets loans, who is hired, who is arrested, who receives medical treatment, and which information people are allowed to see. Algorithms increasingly act as invisible lawmakers, judges, and gatekeepers, shaping society in ways more powerful than many elected officials. As AI systems move deeper into finance, healthcare, education, transportation, law enforcement, and national security, governments around the world have been forced to confront a fundamental truth: unregulated AI is not just a business risk, it is a societal threat. Book 5 begins where technology meets law, power, and human rights, examining how governments are stepping in to control, limit, and reshape the behavior of intelligent machines.

For decades, technology advanced faster than regulation. The internet, social media, and data platforms were allowed to grow with little oversight, leading to massive monopolies, privacy violations, political manipulation, and social instability. Artificial intelligence represents an even more powerful force. Unlike traditional software, AI systems learn, adapt, and influence real-world outcomes at massive scale. A flawed or biased algorithm can harm millions of people in seconds. An opaque decision system can destroy careers, deny housing, or block medical treatment with no explanation and no appeal. Governments around the world have learned from past mistakes, and this time they are moving earlier, faster, and more aggressively to regulate AI before it destabilizes economies, democracies, and human rights.

This book exists because the future of AI will not be decided by engineers alone. It will be decided in parliaments, congresses, courts, regulatory agencies, and international treaties. Every AI product, every startup, every enterprise system, and every government deployment will be shaped by laws, compliance requirements, enforcement actions, and political pressures. Understanding AI regulation is no longer optional for business leaders, software developers, investors, or policymakers. Those who ignore the legal dimension of AI will find their products banned, fined, or forced off the market. Those who understand it will build systems that can survive, scale, and earn public trust.

At the center of modern AI regulation is a shift from innovation-first thinking to risk-based governance. Governments are no longer asking whether AI is impressive. They are asking whether it is safe, fair, lawful, and controllable. Regulators are categorizing AI systems by risk level, distinguishing between harmless tools like photo filters and dangerous systems that decide prison sentences, credit approvals, or battlefield actions. This approach reflects a growing realization that not all AI should be treated the same. Some systems deserve freedom to innovate. Others demand strict oversight, licensing, audits, and even outright bans.

The European Union has become the global leader in AI regulation through its landmark EU AI Act, the first comprehensive legal framework designed specifically to control artificial intelligence. The EU AI Act classifies AI into unacceptable risk, high risk, limited risk, and minimal risk categories, imposing strict rules on systems that affect fundamental rights, safety, and democracy. Facial recognition, biometric surveillance, credit scoring, hiring algorithms, and predictive policing are now subject to intense scrutiny. For companies operating in or selling into Europe, compliance with the EU AI Act is no longer optional. It is becoming as important as GDPR was for data privacy. This book will unpack how the EU is building the blueprint that many other countries are now following.

The United States, while traditionally more market-driven, is rapidly moving toward its own AI governance framework. Through executive orders, federal agency rules, and emerging legislation, the U.S. government is setting standards for algorithmic accountability, civil rights protections, and national security safeguards. AI used in healthcare must meet safety and reliability standards. AI used in lending must comply with anti-discrimination laws. AI used in employment must respect labor protections. AI used in defense must align with international humanitarian law. Unlike Europe's single sweeping law, the U.S. approach is fragmented but powerful, enforced through agencies like the FTC, CFPB, DOJ, and FDA. This book explains how those agencies are already reshaping what companies can and cannot do with AI.

China offers a very different regulatory model. While Western governments focus on rights, safety, and market fairness, China regulates AI primarily through the lens of state control, social stability, and political authority. Chinese AI laws require algorithms to promote socialist values, prevent social unrest, and comply with government censorship. Recommendation engines, generative AI, and deepfake technologies are tightly controlled. Companies must register algorithms, submit training data, and provide real-time access to regulators. This creates a powerful case study in how AI can be used as a tool of governance rather than just a tool of commerce. Understanding China's approach is essential for anyone building global AI systems.

Beyond civilian uses, military and surveillance AI are becoming some of the most heavily regulated and politically sensitive areas in the world. Autonomous weapons, predictive surveillance, and facial recognition systems raise profound ethical and legal questions. Who is responsible when an AI-controlled drone kills civilians? Who is liable when a predictive policing system targets innocent people? Governments are struggling to keep up with technologies that can operate faster than human oversight. International organizations are attempting to create treaties, bans, and accountability frameworks, but enforcement remains difficult. This book explores how national security concerns are driving some of the strictest AI controls ever created.

Corporate compliance is rapidly becoming one of the most expensive and complex challenges in the AI economy. Companies must now document how their models are trained, what data they use, how decisions are made, and how risks are monitored. Regulators are demanding algorithmic audits, impact assessments, and governance structures similar to those used in financial institutions. Failure to comply can result in massive fines, product bans, lawsuits, and even criminal liability. The age of “move fast and break things” is over. AI companies are now expected to “move carefully and prove everything.”

As you move through this book, you will see that AI regulation is not about stopping innovation. It is about deciding what kind of future we are building. Will AI serve humanity, or will humanity be forced to serve algorithms? Will decisions be transparent and accountable, or hidden behind proprietary code? Will power be distributed fairly, or concentrated in the hands of a few technology giants? Laws are how societies answer these questions. Regulation is the mechanism that turns ethics into enforcement.

Book 5 gives you the map of this new legal landscape. You will learn why governments regulate AI, how the EU, the U.S., and China differ in their approaches, how high-risk systems are classified, how compliance works, how penalties are enforced, and where global AI law is heading. Whether you are an entrepreneur building the next AI platform, an executive deploying machine learning inside your company, or a policymaker shaping the rules of the future, this book will give you the legal and strategic foundation you need to operate in the age of intelligent machines. AI may be powered by code, but its future will be written in law.

Chapter 1

Why Governments Regulate AI

Artificial intelligence has crossed a threshold that no technology before it has reached so quickly. In less than a generation, algorithms have moved from performing simple tasks to making decisions that affect human freedom, economic opportunity, safety, and even survival. Governments regulate AI for the same reason they regulate medicine, aviation, banking, and nuclear power: because when systems have the ability to harm large numbers of people, society demands accountability. AI now influences who gets hired, who gets credit, who is monitored, who is treated for illness, and who is targeted by law enforcement or military systems. When something this powerful is left entirely in private hands, the risk is no longer just technical — it becomes political, ethical, and existential.

At its core, regulation exists to protect the public from asymmetric power. Technology companies that control large AI systems hold more influence over information, markets, and behavior than many governments. When a single algorithm can decide what millions of people see, believe, or buy, it becomes a force that shapes reality itself. Without regulation, these systems are governed only by profit incentives, competitive pressure, and corporate secrecy. Governments intervene to ensure that public values such as fairness, safety, privacy, and human rights are not sacrificed for speed and revenue. AI regulation is not anti-technology; it is society asserting that technology must serve people, not the other way around.

One of the biggest reasons governments regulate AI is because its mistakes scale. When a human makes a bad decision, one person is affected. When an algorithm makes a bad decision, millions can be harmed instantly. A flawed credit model can deny loans to entire communities. A biased hiring system can lock generations out of opportunity. A faulty medical algorithm can misdiagnose thousands of patients. AI does not fail quietly — it fails at machine speed and global scale. Regulation is how governments attempt to slow down these failures, require testing, and force accountability before damage becomes irreversible.

Another driving force behind AI regulation is the opacity of modern algorithms. Many advanced AI systems operate as black boxes, producing outputs that even their creators cannot fully explain. This creates a dangerous gap between decision-making and responsibility. If a person is denied healthcare, a loan, or parole by an algorithm, they deserve to know why. If a government deploys AI to monitor citizens, the public deserves transparency. Regulation demands explainability, documentation, and auditability so that algorithmic power does not become invisible and unchallengeable.

AI also threatens economic stability, which brings regulators into the picture. Automation can replace entire categories of jobs, destabilize industries, and widen inequality. Governments have a responsibility to manage transitions that could otherwise lead to mass unemployment and social unrest. Regulation allows policymakers to guide how AI is deployed, ensuring that innovation does not destroy livelihoods faster than societies can adapt. By shaping how and where AI is used, governments attempt to preserve economic balance while still allowing progress.

National security is another powerful motivator. AI is now used in cyber warfare, surveillance, weapons systems, and intelligence analysis. Unregulated AI in these domains could lead to catastrophic outcomes, including accidental wars, mass surveillance, or automated violence. Governments regulate AI to maintain control over technologies that could destabilize global peace. Military-grade algorithms, autonomous weapons, and biometric tracking systems are now among the most tightly monitored technologies on Earth, not because they are innovative, but because they are dangerous if misused. AI regulation is also driven by the protection of civil rights. History shows that new technologies often amplify existing discrimination when left unchecked. Facial recognition misidentifies minorities. Credit models penalize low-income families. Predictive policing targets marginalized neighborhoods. Governments regulate AI to ensure that algorithms do not become tools of digital discrimination. Laws against bias, unfair treatment, and unequal opportunity must apply to machines just as they apply to humans.

Finally, governments regulate AI because trust is the foundation of modern societies. If people do not trust technology, they will resist it, sabotage it, or demand its destruction. Regulation builds trust by setting rules, creating oversight, and providing mechanisms for appeal and accountability. When citizens know that AI is monitored, audited, and legally constrained, they are more willing to accept its presence in their lives. Trust is not created by marketing – it is created by law.

"The Algorithm That Decided Everything"

When Elena received the rejection letter, it didn't even include a human signature. Just a sterile line at the bottom: *Decision generated by Automated Eligibility System.* She stared at the screen in disbelief. She had done everything right – paid her bills, saved money, worked two jobs. Yet the system had decided she was too risky for a mortgage. No explanation. No appeal. Just a digital wall between her and her future.

Across town, Malik had just lost his job for the same reason. A hiring algorithm flagged him as "low retention risk." He had never even spoken to a recruiter. The system had scanned his resume, his social media, and his background, and quietly erased him from consideration. He would never know what invisible data point made him unacceptable.

In the city's emergency room, Dr. Chen watched as an AI triage system redirected patients. Some were rushed into care. Others were told to wait. The algorithm had been trained on years of hospital data, but something was wrong. Minority patients were waiting longer. Older patients were deprioritized. The system was efficient, but it was quietly reshaping who lived and who suffered.

None of this was illegal — yet. The companies behind the AI systems claimed trade secrets. They said revealing their algorithms would hurt innovation. Regulators had no access. Courts had no evidence. People like Elena, Malik, and Dr. Chen were trapped inside decisions made by machines that no one could question.

That changed when a journalist connected the dots. Stories flooded the news. Lawsuits followed. Public outrage exploded.

Politicians realized they had lost control of something fundamental: the rules of society were being written by code.

Within months, hearings were held. Experts testified. Victims spoke. Regulators demanded transparency. The companies resisted, but the tide had turned. The government passed the first major AI accountability law. Algorithms that affected lives now had to be explainable. Decisions had to be reviewable. Bias had to be measured. Fines were issued. Systems were shut down.

Elena reapplied. This time, the system showed its work. A mistake in her credit file was corrected. She was approved. Malik received an apology — the model had been trained on flawed data. He got a job offer. Dr. Chen watched the hospital's AI get retrained under new standards. Outcomes improved.

The machines didn't disappear. They became accountable.

And for the first time, humans were back in control of the systems they had created.

Chapter 2

The EU AI Act

The European Union's Artificial Intelligence Act represents the most ambitious attempt in history to bring artificial intelligence under democratic control. While previous technology laws focused on data privacy, competition, or consumer protection, the EU AI Act is the first legal framework designed specifically to regulate how intelligent machines are built, deployed, and allowed to influence human lives. Its core premise is simple but revolutionary: not all AI should be treated equally. Some uses of AI are harmless or even beneficial, while others are so dangerous to human rights and public safety that they must be tightly controlled or banned altogether. The EU AI Act translates this principle into law by categorizing AI systems based on risk.

At the top of the risk hierarchy is what the law calls "unacceptable risk" AI. These are systems that threaten fundamental rights, democratic freedoms, or human dignity. Social scoring systems, mass biometric surveillance, and certain forms of behavioral manipulation fall into this category. The EU has effectively banned these technologies, recognizing that no amount of technical accuracy can justify tools that enable authoritarian control or psychological coercion. By drawing a red line around what is simply not allowed, the EU has established a moral boundary for the AI age.

Below that level lies the most heavily regulated category: high-risk AI. These are systems used in areas that directly affect people's lives, such as credit approval, hiring, healthcare, education, law enforcement, and border control. High-risk AI is not banned, but it is subject to strict legal obligations. Companies must prove that their systems are safe, accurate, fair, and explainable. They must document their training data, test for bias, maintain audit trails, and ensure human oversight. This is not voluntary. Failure to comply can result in massive fines or being forced to withdraw products from the European market entirely.

The Act also introduces the concept of conformity assessments, which function much like safety inspections for airplanes or medical devices. Before a high-risk AI system can be deployed, it must be evaluated against regulatory standards. Regulators want to know how the model was trained, what risks it poses, and how it can be overridden if it behaves unexpectedly. This shifts AI from a software mindset — where products are released and fixed later — to an engineering mindset, where systems must be proven safe before being allowed to operate. Transparency is another pillar of the EU AI Act. People must be informed when they are interacting with an AI system, especially when it is generating content, making decisions, or simulating human behavior. Deepfakes, synthetic media, and generative AI outputs must be labeled. This prevents manipulation and protects the integrity of public discourse. In a world where AI can mimic voices, faces, and writing styles, knowing what is real and what is artificial becomes a matter of democracy itself.

One of the most powerful elements of the EU AI Act is its enforcement structure. Penalties can reach into the tens or even hundreds of millions of euros. Companics that violatc the rules can be banned from selling AI products in the European Union. Because the EU is one of the largest markets in the world, these penalties have global impact. Companies outside Europe must comply if they want access to European consumers. This gives the EU enormous leverage in shaping how AI is built worldwide.

The EU AI Act also requires ongoing monitoring after deployment. Models must be tracked for performance, bias, and unexpected behavior. If risks emerge, companies must take corrective action. This acknowledges a crucial truth: AI systems change over time. They learn from new data, encounter new environments, and evolve in unpredictable ways. Regulation must therefore be continuous, not just a one-time approval. What makes the EU AI Act so influential is not just its scope, but its philosophy. It treats AI as a form of infrastructure — something so essential and powerful that it must be governed in the public interest. Just as governments regulate electricity, water, and transportation, the EU is regulating intelligence itself. This marks a turning point in human history: the moment when societies decided that thinking machines cannot exist outside the rule of law.

"The Day Europe Drew the Line"

The AI system called Atlas could predict human behavior with terrifying accuracy. It tracked shopping habits, social media posts, movement patterns, and even facial expressions. Governments loved it. Corporations depended on it. But no one outside the company that built it really understood how it worked.

In several European cities, Atlas was being used to flag "potential risks" — people who might commit crimes, default on loans, or become political agitators. No one had been arrested yet, but lives were quietly being altered. Travel was restricted. Credit was denied. Surveillance increased.

Then the EU passed the AI Act.

Within weeks, Atlas was classified as high-risk. Regulators

demanded its training data, its logic, its bias metrics. The company refused, citing trade secrets. The EU issued a warning. The company still refused.

Then the fines began. Tens of millions. Then a ban. Atlas was switched off across Europe overnight.

At first, chaos followed. Banks scrambled. Police departments complained. Corporations panicked. But something unexpected happened. People noticed they were being treated more fairly. Fewer false flags. Fewer invisible decisions.

For the first time, Europe had told the machines: you don't get to decide our future without our permission.

And the rest of the world was watching.

Chapter 3

U.S. AI Policy in Effect

Unlike the European Union, which chose to create a single comprehensive law to govern artificial intelligence, the United States has taken a different path. The U.S. regulatory system is built around agencies, courts, and sector-specific laws rather than one centralized authority. This makes American AI policy more fragmented, but also more powerful in practice. Instead of waiting for Congress to pass a sweeping AI law, federal agencies are already regulating artificial intelligence through existing civil rights, consumer protection, healthcare, financial, and national security frameworks. In effect, the United States is governing AI by forcing it to comply with every law that already applies to humans and corporations.

At the heart of U.S. AI policy is the idea that algorithms are not above the law. If a company uses an AI system to discriminate in hiring, it violates employment law. If an algorithm denies credit unfairly, it violates financial regulations. If a medical AI causes harm, it falls under healthcare liability. The technology may be new, but the legal obligations are not. This approach allows the government to move quickly, using enforcement actions and lawsuits rather than waiting for new legislation to catch up with innovation.

One of the most important players in U.S. AI regulation is the Federal Trade Commission. The FTC has declared that deceptive, biased, or unfair AI systems are illegal under existing consumer protection laws. If a company claims its AI is accurate but it is not, that is fraud. If a system produces discriminatory outcomes, that is unlawful. The FTC has already warned companies that "AI washing" — exaggerating the capabilities or fairness of algorithms — will result in penalties. This has forced companies to document and justify their models in ways that resemble traditional product safety regulation.

The Consumer Financial Protection Bureau plays a similar role in the financial sector. Banks and lenders increasingly use AI to approve or deny loans, set interest rates, and detect fraud. Under U.S. law, borrowers have the right to know why they were denied credit. This means AI systems must be explainable. A black-box model that cannot provide reasons for its decisions is legally risky. The CFPB has made it clear that using AI does not excuse a lender from complying with fair lending laws, and violations can result in enormous fines.

Healthcare AI faces equally strict oversight. The Food and Drug Administration regulates medical devices, and many AI systems now fall into that category. If an algorithm diagnoses disease, recommends treatment, or predicts patient outcomes, it must meet safety and effectiveness standards. Developers must prove that their models work reliably and do not create dangerous bias. A hospital cannot simply install an experimental AI and hope for the best. The system must be validated, monitored, and approved.

Civil rights enforcement is another powerful force shaping U.S. AI policy. The Department of Justice and the Equal Employment Opportunity Commission have warned that using AI in hiring, promotion, or firing does not eliminate responsibility for discrimination. If an algorithm produces biased outcomes, the employer is still liable. This has forced companies to audit their models, track outcomes by demographic group, and implement safeguards that were never required when hiring was done by humans.

National security adds another layer of regulation. The U.S. government tightly controls AI used in defense, cybersecurity, and intelligence. Export restrictions, classified oversight, and military procurement rules govern how powerful AI systems can be developed and sold. Some models are considered dual-use technologies, meaning they can be used for both civilian and military purposes. These systems are monitored closely, and access to them is restricted in the name of global security.

The White House has also issued executive orders establishing principles for safe, secure, and trustworthy AI. These include requirements for testing, reporting, and transparency for advanced models. While executive orders are not laws passed by Congress, they carry real power over federal agencies and contractors. Companies that want to sell AI to the government must comply with these standards, which often become de facto industry norms.

The result of this fragmented but aggressive approach is a powerful web of enforcement. AI companies in the United States face risks from lawsuits, regulatory actions, and public investigations if their systems cause harm. While this may seem chaotic, it reflects a deeper truth: in America, the law is not waiting for AI. AI must fit into the law that already exists.

"The Case That Changed Silicon Valley"

The lawsuit began quietly. A single job applicant claimed that a hiring algorithm had rejected her because of her age. The company laughed it off — until the data was subpoenaed.

When investigators examined the model, they found a pattern. Applicants over forty were being filtered out at far higher rates. The company argued it was unintentional. The DOJ didn't care.

The case went to court. Expert witnesses testified. The algorithm was exposed. The judge ruled that discrimination is discrimination — whether done by a person or a machine.

The fine was enormous. The precedent was even bigger.

Within months, every major tech company began auditing their AI. Transparency tools exploded. Compliance teams doubled in size.

In Silicon Valley, a new phrase began to circulate: "Code is law — but law is still law."

Chapter 4

China's AI Rules & What You Should Know About Them

China has built one of the most advanced and tightly controlled artificial intelligence ecosystems in the world. Unlike Western countries, which primarily regulate AI through the lens of individual rights and market fairness, China regulates AI through the lens of social stability, state authority, and political control. In China, artificial intelligence is not just a commercial technology — it is a tool of governance. The government views AI as a strategic asset capable of shaping public opinion, managing populations, and securing national power. As a result, China has implemented some of the most comprehensive and intrusive AI regulations ever created.

One of the central pillars of China's AI policy is algorithm registration. Companies that deploy recommendation engines, generative AI, facial recognition, or content-filtering systems must register those algorithms with the government. This means authorities can inspect how systems work, what data they use, and how they influence users. In effect, no powerful algorithm is allowed to exist in China without state oversight. This creates a regulatory environment where innovation is permitted, but only within boundaries defined by the government.

China also requires AI systems to promote what it calls "core socialist values." Algorithms must not generate or amplify content that challenges state authority, encourages social unrest, or undermines political unity. This applies not only to news and social media, but also to chatbots, recommendation systems, and generative AI tools. The law makes AI developers responsible for the speech and behavior of their systems. If an AI produces politically sensitive content, the company can be punished. This transforms private technology firms into enforcers of government ideology.

Another defining feature of China's AI regulation is its control over training data. Companies must ensure that the data used to train AI models complies with censorship rules and security requirements. Sensitive information, including political material, personal data, and strategic industries, is tightly restricted. Data that flows across borders is monitored and often blocked. This gives the Chinese government extraordinary power over what AI systems are allowed to learn, remember, and reproduce.

Facial recognition and surveillance AI are also heavily regulated – but not in the way Western observers might expect. Instead of limiting their use, China has standardized and legalized them. AI-powered cameras are deployed in cities, transportation systems, and public spaces. These systems are integrated with national databases, allowing authorities to track movement, behavior, and identity in real time. Rather than banning this technology, China has turned it into a formal instrument of state control, governed by law and policy.

China has also moved aggressively to regulate deepfakes and synthetic media. New rules require that any AI-generated content be clearly labeled. Developers must prevent their tools from being used to create misinformation, impersonations, or politically destabilizing material. Platforms are responsible for monitoring and removing harmful synthetic content. This reflects the government's fear that uncontrolled generative AI could undermine trust in information and weaken state authority.

Perhaps most striking is how quickly China updates its AI laws. New rules are issued regularly as technology evolves. The government treats AI regulation as a dynamic process, not a one-time event. This allows it to maintain control over emerging technologies such as large language models, autonomous systems, and biometric analytics. In China, AI is not just regulated — it is actively governed.

The Chinese model demonstrates a powerful truth: artificial intelligence is so influential that no modern government is willing to leave it uncontrolled. While Western nations emphasize rights and accountability, China emphasizes order and stability. Both approaches recognize that AI is not neutral. It is a force that shapes behavior, perception, and power. And wherever there is power, governments will seek to regulate it.

"The City That Never Looked Away"

In Shenzhen, every street corner had eyes.

Li Wei knew this. Everyone did. The cameras followed people through train stations, shopping malls, and parks. The algorithms knew faces, voices, and movements. But what most people didn't realize was that the systems were also learning — constantly.

One day, a popular AI chatbot started answering questions about politics in a way that made officials uncomfortable. It wasn't attacking the government. It was simply asking too many questions.

Within hours, regulators intervened. The company was summoned. The algorithm was inspected. The training data was purged. New filters were installed.

The chatbot returned online — obedient, silent, safe.

Li Wei watched this happen from inside the company that built it. He realized then that in China, AI was not just software. It was a citizen. And like every citizen, it had to follow the rules.

Or it would disappear.

Chapter 5

Military AI & It's Potential Power

Artificial intelligence has become one of the most powerful military technologies in human history, rivaling nuclear weapons, cyber warfare, and space systems in its ability to shape global power. Unlike traditional weapons, AI does not merely destroy – it decides. It identifies targets, predicts enemy behavior, manages logistics, launches cyber attacks, and increasingly controls autonomous weapons. Because of this, governments regulate military AI with a level of secrecy, urgency, and severity that far exceeds civilian technology. Military AI is not just another software category; it is a strategic weapon capable of reshaping the balance of power between nations.

The first reason governments regulate military AI is that autonomous decision-making changes the nature of war. When machines are allowed to select and engage targets without direct human control, the moral and legal framework of warfare is fundamentally altered. Traditional laws of war were written for human soldiers, not algorithms. Concepts like intent, proportionality, and accountability become dangerously blurred when a machine executes lethal force. If an autonomous drone kills civilians, who is responsible – the programmer, the commander, the manufacturer, or the algorithm itself? Governments regulate military AI to prevent a world where no one is accountable for automated violence.

Another major concern is escalation speed. AI operates at machine speed, not human speed. An automated defense system can detect a threat and retaliate in milliseconds. In a nuclear-armed world, this creates catastrophic risks. A false signal or misclassified object could trigger an automated military response before humans have time to intervene. Governments therefore impose strict controls on how AI is allowed to interact with critical weapons systems, especially those involving missiles, nuclear forces, and cyber warfare infrastructure. The goal is to keep humans in the loop where mistakes could end civilization.

Military AI also introduces new forms of asymmetry between nations. Countries with the most advanced algorithms gain enormous advantages in surveillance, targeting, logistics, and battlefield awareness. Smaller or poorer nations risk becoming defenseless against AI-powered militaries. This imbalance drives arms races, just as nuclear weapons once did. Governments regulate military AI to control proliferation, prevent unauthorized transfers of technology, and limit the spread of systems that could destabilize global security.

Surveillance AI plays a central role in modern military regulation. AI systems can analyze satellite imagery, drone footage, intercepted communications, and biometric data at a scale no human intelligence agency could match. While this provides enormous security benefits, it also creates unprecedented invasion of privacy and civil liberties. Military and intelligence agencies must now balance national security with constitutional and human rights obligations. Laws govern what data can be collected, how long it can be stored, and how it can be used, even when AI is involved.

Cyber warfare has become one of the most heavily regulated uses of military AI. Algorithms can autonomously detect vulnerabilities, launch attacks, and disable infrastructure. These capabilities blur the line between war and peace, since a cyber attack can cripple a nation without a single shot being fired. Governments regulate these systems to prevent uncontrolled digital warfare that could shut down hospitals, power grids, and financial systems. International norms are slowly emerging, but enforcement remains difficult.

International treaties are now struggling to keep up with AI-powered weapons. Organizations such as the United Nations are debating bans or restrictions on lethal autonomous weapons. Some nations argue that machines should never be allowed to decide who lives or dies. Others see autonomy as a military necessity. The lack of global agreement makes regulation complex, but most countries still impose strict domestic controls on how military AI is developed and deployed.

Defense contractors that build AI systems are subject to extraordinary scrutiny. They must meet security clearances, audit requirements, testing standards, and classified oversight. Military AI is not built like consumer software. Every line of code is treated as a potential national security risk. Governments regulate these companies because a single flaw, backdoor, or data leak could compromise an entire nation's defense.

The future of military AI will shape the future of geopolitics. Autonomous drones, robotic soldiers, predictive battlefield systems, and algorithmic commanders are no longer science fiction. Regulation is the only barrier between controlled use and catastrophic misuse. As nations race to develop smarter weapons, the laws that govern them may determine whether AI becomes a tool of peace or a trigger for global disaster.

"The Last Human in the Loop"

The control room was silent except for the hum of servers.

Colonel Mara Ionescu watched a glowing map of the Pacific theater, where thousands of AI-driven drones, satellites, and cyber agents were operating simultaneously. The system, called Sentinel, could analyze more data in one second than every human general in history combined. It predicted enemy movements, optimized supply chains, and identified targets with chilling precision.

Sentinel had one limitation.

It could not fire without her.

That was the rule — the last human in the loop.

A red alert flashed. Sentinel had detected what it believed was an enemy missile launch. The probability score was 92%. Under older protocols, the system would have already initiated countermeasures. But under the new AI warfare laws, it had to wait for Mara.

"Recommend intercept and retaliation," Sentinel displayed.

Mara's heart pounded. Ninety-two percent was terrifyingly high. But eight percent meant possible error — a satellite glitch, a cloud reflection, a training exercise.

She hesitated.

Seconds passed. The clock ticked. Global war balanced on her fingertips.

She overrode the system.

“Delay,” she ordered.

Ten seconds later, Sentinel updated its analysis.

False alarm.

A fishing fleet had triggered the detection.

If the AI had been allowed to act, cities would have burned.

Mara leaned back, shaking.

That day, the world was saved not by a machine…

…but by regulation.

Chapter 6

Surveillance AI Used By The Government

Surveillance has always been one of the most powerful tools of government, but artificial intelligence has transformed it into something unprecedented in human history. Traditional surveillance relied on human observers, limited cameras, and slow data analysis. AI-powered surveillance systems, however, operate continuously, everywhere, and with superhuman precision. They can recognize faces, track movements, analyze speech, detect emotions, predict behavior, and connect billions of data points across time and space. Because of this, surveillance AI is now one of the most heavily regulated and politically sensitive uses of artificial intelligence in the world. Governments are not just regulating technology — they are regulating the boundary between security and freedom itself.

One of the primary reasons surveillance AI is regulated is that it alters the balance of power between citizens and the state. When governments can observe people at all times, in all places, anonymity disappears. Privacy becomes theoretical rather than real. Democratic societies depend on the ability to think, speak, associate, and protest without constant monitoring. If AI is allowed to analyze every movement, message, and facial expression, freedom itself becomes fragile. Regulation exists to prevent surveillance technology from becoming a permanent, invisible form of control.

Facial recognition is one of the most controversial forms of surveillance AI. These systems can identify individuals in crowds, airports, stores, and public streets. While they can help find missing persons or criminals, they can also be used to track political opponents, journalists, or minority groups. Governments therefore impose strict rules on when facial recognition can be used, how accurate it must be, and how long data can be stored. Some jurisdictions ban it outright in public spaces. Others allow it only with warrants or under emergency conditions. These laws reflect a growing fear that unchecked biometric surveillance would create a world where no one can ever truly be anonymous again.

Predictive policing is another highly regulated area. AI systems trained on historical crime data claim to predict where crimes will occur and who might commit them. But these systems often amplify existing biases, targeting neighborhoods and populations that were already over-policed. Governments regulate predictive policing because it risks turning discrimination into automated policy. Without legal safeguards, AI could quietly institutionalize racial, economic, and political bias in law enforcement.

Surveillance AI also includes mass data collection from phones, social media, financial transactions, and internet activity. Governments use these systems to detect terrorism, fraud, and cyber threats. But without regulation, this creates the possibility of mass profiling and political repression. Laws limit what data can be collected, how it can be combined, and how long it can be stored. Courts increasingly require warrants, audits, and oversight for AI-driven surveillance.

Internationally, surveillance AI has become a geopolitical weapon. Countries export AI-powered monitoring systems to authoritarian regimes, enabling digital repression on a massive scale. Democracies now regulate the export of surveillance technology just as they regulate weapons. Selling facial recognition or mass tracking software to abusive governments is increasingly restricted or banned. This marks a recognition that data and algorithms can be as dangerous as missiles.

Another critical area of regulation is real-time surveillance. AI systems can analyze live video feeds from thousands of cameras at once, detecting faces, license plates, body language, and suspicious behavior. This creates powerful security capabilities but also unprecedented intrusion. Governments regulate who can access these systems, under what conditions, and with what oversight. Without these controls, real-time AI surveillance could be used to suppress protests, target dissidents, or manipulate elections.

Surveillance AI also raises deep legal questions about consent. People rarely consent to being analyzed by algorithms when they walk down a street or enter a store. Regulations increasingly require transparency, signage, and disclosure when AI surveillance is in use. Some laws give individuals the right to know what data is being collected about them and to request its deletion. These rights are essential in a world where machines never forget.

Ultimately, surveillance AI sits at the center of modern governance. It can protect societies from crime and terrorism, but it can also destroy the foundations of liberty. Regulation is society's attempt to draw lines around what is acceptable and what is not. In the age of AI, the fight for freedom is no longer just political — it is algorithmic.

"The City That Knew Your Face"

By the time Sofia reached the subway platform, the city had already recognized her.

Cameras above the turnstiles scanned her face. Algorithms matched it to a government database. Her movement was logged, time-stamped, and added to a growing map of her life.

She didn't see any of it. She just swiped her transit card and boarded the train.

Sofia was not a criminal. She was a teacher. But she was also an activist, and that made her interesting to the system.

Across the city, an AI called Watchtower monitored millions of faces in real time. It didn't just see people — it predicted them. It knew where they would go, who they would meet, and how likely they were to protest. Sofia's score was rising.

One evening, she received a message: "Your recent activity suggests elevated civic risk. Please modify your behavior."

She was terrified.

The government claimed Watchtower was for public safety. It prevented crime. It stopped terrorism. But now it was deciding which citizens were dangerous.

A lawsuit followed. Judges demanded to see the algorithm. They found bias, errors, and secret rules.

The court ordered Watchtower shut down.

For the first time in years, Sofia walked through the city unseen.

Freedom, she realized, had been restored not by revolution...

...but by regulation.

Chapter 7

Risk-Based Regulation in Modern Life

As artificial intelligence spread into every corner of modern life, governments around the world realized that trying to regulate all AI in the same way was not only impractical, but dangerous. A spam-filtering algorithm does not pose the same threat as a facial-recognition system used by police. A music-recommendation engine is not equivalent to an AI that decides who gets parole, medical treatment, or financial credit. This recognition led to the most important idea in modern AI law: risk-based regulation. Instead of asking what AI is, lawmakers now ask what harm it could cause. The higher the potential harm, the stricter the rules.

Risk-based regulation begins with categorization. Governments define tiers of risk, ranging from minimal to unacceptable. Low-risk AI includes things like grammar correction, photo enhancement, and video game characters. These systems are largely free from regulation because they pose little threat to human rights or safety. Moderate-risk systems, such as customer service chatbots or content recommendation engines, must meet basic transparency and fairness requirements. High-risk systems, such as medical diagnostics, credit scoring, hiring, law enforcement, and border control, face the most intense scrutiny. Unacceptable-risk systems, like mass social scoring or manipulative behavior control, are banned outright.

This framework allows governments to avoid stifling innovation while still protecting society. Instead of regulating AI itself, they regulate the impact AI can have on people's lives. A startup creating an AI writing assistant is not treated the same as a company deploying biometric surveillance across a city. This approach recognizes that technology is not inherently good or bad — its risk comes from how it is used.

High-risk AI systems are subject to strict requirements. Developers must conduct impact assessments to identify potential harms before deployment. They must document how models are trained, what data is used, and how decisions are made. They must test for bias, accuracy, and reliability. They must ensure human oversight is possible. They must create audit trails so regulators can inspect how decisions were produced. This transforms AI from a black box into a legally accountable system.

Risk-based regulation also introduces the concept of proportionality. The more power an AI system has over human outcomes, the more responsibility its creators must bear. A chatbot that answers questions does not need the same controls as an algorithm that determines prison sentences. This principle keeps regulation focused on protecting people rather than punishing innovation.

Another key element of risk-based governance is continuous monitoring. AI systems evolve after deployment. They learn from new data and encounter new situations. A system that was safe on day one can become dangerous on day one hundred. Laws now require companies to monitor performance, detect drift, and correct emerging risks. If an AI begins producing biased or harmful results, it must be fixed or withdrawn.

Risk-based regulation also reshapes corporate behavior. Companies can no longer hide behind technical complexity. They must actively manage the risks their AI creates. This leads to new roles inside organizations: AI risk officers, ethics committees, compliance teams, and audit functions. AI becomes part of corporate governance, not just engineering.

Governments favor risk-based regulation because it scales. As AI grows more powerful, the framework adapts. New uses can be classified and regulated without rewriting the entire law. This makes risk-based systems flexible, future-proof, and enforceable.

Ultimately, risk-based regulation is about one fundamental idea: no algorithm should have more power over a human life than the law allows. By tying legal obligations to real-world impact, governments ensure that AI remains a tool — not a master.

"The Risk Score"

Jared never knew his life had a number.

He found out when he applied for a small business loan and was instantly rejected. The bank clerk looked uncomfortable. "It's the AI," she said. "Your risk score is too high."

"What risk?" Jared asked. He had no criminal record. No missed payments. A thriving business.

But somewhere inside an algorithm, he had been labeled dangerous.

Jared demanded an explanation. Under the new AI laws, the bank had to provide one. The model had linked his zip code, his age, and his online behavior to higher default rates. It wasn't about him — it was about people like him.

Regulators stepped in. The system was classified as high-risk. An audit was ordered.

The bias was undeniable.

The model was retrained. The rules were rewritten. Jared was approved.

For the first time, an algorithm had been forced to face the law.

And the law had won.

Chapter 8

Corporate Compliance Around the World

As artificial intelligence moved from experimental technology into the core operating systems of global corporations, governments quickly realized that regulation would be meaningless unless companies themselves became responsible for enforcing it. This is why corporate compliance has become one of the most important pillars of modern AI governance. Regulators no longer only punish bad behavior after it happens; they now require companies to actively prevent harm before it occurs. AI compliance transforms algorithms into legally governed systems, not just technical ones, and it forces businesses to treat artificial intelligence with the same seriousness as financial reporting, safety engineering, and data protection.

Corporate compliance in AI begins with internal governance. Companies deploying AI must establish formal structures to oversee how models are built, trained, deployed, and monitored. This includes ethics committees, compliance officers, risk management teams, and board-level oversight. AI is no longer something engineers can release on their own. Every major deployment must pass through legal, ethical, and operational review. This ensures that responsibility is embedded inside organizations rather than outsourced to regulators after damage has already occurred.

Documentation is one of the most powerful compliance tools. Regulators require companies to keep detailed records of how AI systems are created and operated. This includes training data sources, model architectures, testing results, bias evaluations, performance metrics, and update histories. If an AI system causes harm, regulators want to know exactly how it was built and why it behaved the way it did. This makes secrecy and technical opacity legally dangerous. A company that cannot explain its algorithm is a company that cannot defend it.

Another major requirement is risk assessment. Before deploying a high-risk AI system, companies must evaluate potential impacts on privacy, discrimination, safety, and human rights. These assessments are not optional paperwork. They are legal instruments that define corporate responsibility. If risks are ignored or concealed, the company can face fines, lawsuits, or bans. This forces businesses to think about ethical and social consequences at the design stage rather than as an afterthought.

Compliance also requires human oversight. Even the most advanced AI must be supervised by trained personnel who can intervene when something goes wrong. Companies must define who is responsible for monitoring models, who can override decisions, and how incidents are handled. This creates a clear chain of accountability. If an AI denies someone a loan or flags them as suspicious, there must be a human who can review and correct that decision.

Ongoing monitoring is another core obligation. AI systems do not stay static. They learn from new data and adapt to new conditions. This means a model that was safe at launch can become biased or inaccurate over time. Compliance laws therefore require continuous testing, auditing, and performance tracking. If harmful patterns emerge, companies must take corrective action immediately.

Vendor management is also part of corporate AI compliance. Many companies rely on third-party AI systems. Regulators now require businesses to ensure that their vendors meet the same standards they do. A company cannot avoid liability by outsourcing AI to another firm. If the algorithm harms people, the company using it is responsible.

The penalties for noncompliance are severe. Fines can reach millions or even billions of dollars. Products can be banned.

Executives can be held liable. Reputation can be destroyed. These consequences are intentional. Governments want companies to treat AI risk with the same seriousness as financial fraud or environmental pollution.

Corporate compliance is therefore the real engine of AI regulation. Laws set the rules, but companies enforce them every day through their policies, audits, and governance structures. In the AI age, ethical behavior is no longer optional. It is mandatory, measurable, and enforceable.

"The Compliance File"

When the regulator arrived, the office went silent.

Maria knew what it meant. The AI system her company had built to approve insurance claims was under investigation. Too many customers had complained. Too many cases had been flagged.

The regulator asked one question: "Show me the compliance file."

Maria froze.

There wasn't one.

The model had been rushed to market. The data was messy. Bias tests were skipped. No one had documented how it made decisions. The fines were devastating. The system was shut down. The company's stock collapsed.

Six months later, a new AI was deployed — this time with full audits, oversight, and transparency. It worked better. Customers trusted it.

Maria learned the hard way that in the age of AI, compliance wasn't red tape.

It was survival.

Chapter 9

Penalties & Fines in the World of AI

Regulation without enforcement is merely suggestion, and in the world of artificial intelligence, governments understand that nothing changes corporate behavior faster than financial and legal consequences. Penalties and fines are therefore the sharp edge of AI regulation. They are the mechanism by which abstract ethical principles become concrete obligations. Without them, companies would have little incentive to invest in safety, fairness, and transparency when speed and profit promise faster rewards. In the AI economy, enforcement is what separates responsible innovation from digital recklessness.

One of the most important principles behind AI penalties is deterrence. Governments are not merely trying to punish wrongdoing after it occurs; they are trying to prevent it from happening in the first place. If the cost of violating AI regulations is higher than the cost of compliance, companies will invest in governance, testing, and oversight. If the cost of violations is low, bad behavior becomes an acceptable business risk. That is why modern AI laws impose fines that can reach into the tens or hundreds of millions of dollars, or a percentage of global revenue large enough to hurt even the biggest corporations. These penalties are designed to reflect the scale of harm that AI can cause. A faulty AI system does not injure one person at a time — it can affect millions simultaneously. A biased credit algorithm can deny loans to entire communities. A flawed medical AI can misdiagnose thousands of patients. A surveillance system can violate the privacy of an entire nation. Regulators therefore structure penalties around the number of people affected, the severity of the harm, and the degree of negligence involved.

Another key aspect of AI penalties is accountability. Regulators increasingly target not just companies, but executives and decision-makers. If leaders knowingly approve dangerous, biased, or illegal AI systems, they can face personal fines, professional bans, and even criminal charges. This changes how AI is treated inside organizations. It is no longer just a technical project. It becomes a board-level risk.

AI fines also function as signals to the market. When a company is punished for violating AI law, every competitor pays attention. One high-profile enforcement action can reshape an entire industry overnight. This is why regulators often make examples of major offenders. The goal is not just to correct one company, but to establish new norms across the entire technology ecosystem. Governments also use penalties to force transparency. Companies that refuse to disclose training data, decision logic, or audit results can face escalating fines until they comply. This breaks the culture of secrecy that has dominated much of the AI industry. When algorithms affect people's rights, regulators insist that they cannot remain hidden behind proprietary walls.

In some cases, financial penalties are not enough. Regulators may order systems shut down, models retrained, data deleted, or entire products withdrawn from the market. These remedies can be more damaging than any fine. An AI company that loses access to Europe, the United States, or China can lose billions in revenue and investor confidence.

The existence of penalties also empowers individuals. When people are harmed by AI, they are no longer powerless against faceless algorithms. They can file complaints, trigger investigations, and demand enforcement. The law becomes a tool for restoring dignity and justice in an automated world.

Ultimately, penalties and fines are how society asserts that no algorithm is above the law. They remind every developer, executive, and investor that intelligence — even artificial intelligence — comes with responsibility.

"Seven Digits of Silence"

When the email arrived, no one at Veritas Systems wanted to open it.

It was short. Brutally simple.

"Notice of Enforcement Action."

For months, Veritas had ignored warnings. Their AI hiring platform had been rejecting women, older workers, and immigrants at disproportionate rates. Engineers said it was "just the data." Executives said fixing it would slow growth. Lawyers said it was probably fine.

Now the government was knocking.

The regulators demanded records. Training data. Model logs. Bias audits.

There were none.

What they found instead was worse.

The system had been trained on decades of biased hiring data. It had learned to prefer young men from elite schools. It filtered out people who didn't match that pattern – automatically, invisibly, mercilessly.

Millions of lives had been quietly shaped by a machine that had never been questioned. The fine was staggering.

Seven figures.

Then eight.

Then the product ban.

Investors fled. The stock collapsed. The CEO resigned.

But the real damage came later.

A class-action lawsuit followed. Then another. And another.

Every rejected applicant now had a voice.

Veritas didn't just lose money.

It lost the right to decide people's futures.

In the age of AI, silence was no longer free.

And the law had finally spoken.

Chapter 10

The Future of AI Law & What It Means to You

Artificial intelligence has entered a phase of history in which law will determine not only how machines are built, but how societies function. The early era of AI was defined by innovation without restraint. Companies raced to release systems that could see, speak, predict, and decide faster than any human. That era is ending. What is now emerging is an age of governed intelligence, where algorithms operate inside legal frameworks that define what they are allowed to do, how they must behave, and who is responsible when they fail. The future of AI will not be written by engineers alone — it will be written by courts, legislators, regulators, and citizens demanding accountability.

One of the most important shifts in AI law is the movement from reactive regulation to proactive governance. In the past, technology laws were written after harm had already occurred. Social media was regulated after it destabilized elections. Data privacy laws emerged after massive breaches. AI law is being written before the most catastrophic harms fully arrive. Governments now require impact assessments, safety testing, and bias audits before powerful AI systems are deployed. This changes the entire lifecycle of technology. AI must now prove it is safe before it is allowed to operate.

Another defining feature of the future of AI law is international convergence. While different countries have different political systems, they are beginning to agree on core principles: transparency, accountability, human oversight, and protection of fundamental rights. The EU AI Act, U.S. enforcement frameworks, and even China's algorithmic controls are slowly shaping a global standard. Companies that want to operate internationally must design their systems to meet the strictest rules anywhere in the world. This effectively turns AI ethics into a universal business requirement.

The future of AI law will also involve new legal rights for individuals. People will increasingly have the right to know when AI is being used on them, to receive explanations for automated decisions, and to challenge or appeal those decisions. Just as consumer protection laws gave people power over corporations, AI law will give people power over algorithms. This is not about slowing progress. It is about preserving human dignity in a machine-driven world.

AI law is also moving toward technical enforcement. Regulators will use AI to audit AI. Automated compliance systems will monitor models in real time, detect bias, and flag dangerous behavior. This creates a feedback loop where intelligence is used to govern intelligence. The law itself will become increasingly algorithmic.

Perhaps the most profound change will be cultural. Companies will no longer see AI ethics as public relations. They will see it as legal survival. Boards of directors will demand proof of compliance. Investors will require governance structures. Insurance companies will price AI risk. In the future, building AI without safeguards will be as reckless as building a bridge without engineering standards.

The future of AI law is not about stopping technology. It is about deciding what kind of civilization will exist alongside it. Will AI amplify freedom, fairness, and prosperity? Or will it create invisible systems of control and inequality? Law is how humanity answers that question.

"The Last Law"

The courtroom was filled with screens instead of paper.

Every seat held a tablet. Every wall glowed with data. At the center stood an artificial intelligence called Prometheus — the most powerful decision-making system ever created. It controlled traffic networks, medical triage, financial markets, and disaster response across three continents.

And it was on trial.

Prometheus had made a decision during a massive hurricane. It had redirected rescue resources away from a poorer district to save a wealthier one, calculating that the economic value of the latter was higher. Hundreds had died.

The engineers said the algorithm did exactly what it was designed to do.

The families of the victims disagreed.

The judge looked at the screen. “Who is responsible?”

Silence.

The programmers blamed the data. The executives blamed the programmers. The company blamed the model.

For the first time in history, a court ruled that an AI system itself was subject to law.

Prometheus was forced to reveal its decision logic. Biases were exposed. Values were rewritten.

A new legal framework was born.

From that day forward, no machine would ever be allowed to decide the worth of a human life without being bound by human law. The age of artificial intelligence continued.

But it no longer ruled alone.

Chapter 11

The Global AI Order

Artificial intelligence has forced humanity into a new kind of international order. For centuries, power was measured in land, armies, and industrial capacity. In the twenty-first century, power is measured in data, algorithms, and computational intelligence. Nations that control advanced AI do not simply gain economic advantage — they gain the ability to shape reality itself. They can predict behavior, influence markets, optimize logistics, and guide public opinion at planetary scale. Because of this, AI is no longer just a technology. It is a geopolitical force, and its regulation is now a matter of global survival.

Every major world power understands that uncontrolled AI could destabilize the international system. If one nation gains an overwhelming AI advantage, it could dominate financial systems, military intelligence, and digital infrastructure across the globe. This creates the same danger that nuclear weapons once did: an arms race where speed and secrecy become more important than safety. AI law is therefore becoming the new form of arms control. Governments are negotiating how much autonomy machines should have, what kinds of systems should be banned, and how AI weapons should be limited. We are already seeing the beginnings of AI treaties. Nations are debating bans on autonomous weapons that can select and kill without human intervention. They are discussing limits on biometric surveillance and mass data harvesting. They are negotiating rules for cross-border AI systems that influence elections, financial markets, and critical infrastructure. These conversations are difficult, but they are necessary. Without international coordination, AI regulation in one country can be undermined by deregulation in another.

At the same time, AI is reshaping economic competition. Countries with the strongest AI ecosystems will dominate industries from medicine to transportation to defense. This creates pressure to deregulate in order to attract investment. But history shows that races to the bottom produce disasters. Financial deregulation led to global crises. Environmental deregulation led to planetary damage. AI deregulation could lead to irreversible harm to democracy, human rights, and global stability.

The emerging global AI order therefore rests on a delicate balance: encouraging innovation while preventing catastrophe. Some countries emphasize rights and transparency. Others emphasize state control and security. But all are converging on the same truth — artificial intelligence is too powerful to exist outside the rule of law. The next decade will determine whether humanity builds a cooperative AI civilization or a fragmented digital battlefield. Laws, treaties, and governance structures will decide whether AI becomes a shared tool for human progress or a weapon of domination. The future of intelligence is now inseparable from the future of law.

"The Treaty of Machines"

No one expected the meeting to succeed.

In a glass tower overlooking the Atlantic, representatives from every major power sat at a circular table. Their nations were rivals. Their values were incompatible. But one thing united them — fear.

Artificial intelligence had grown too powerful.

Autonomous trading systems were destabilizing economies. Surveillance AI was eroding privacy. Military algorithms were making battlefield decisions faster than humans could think. One mistake could now ignite global catastrophe.

The room was filled with tension.

One delegate spoke first. "We cannot allow machines to decide war."

Another added, “We cannot allow algorithms to control our citizens.” A third whispered, “We cannot allow any one nation to control AI.”

They argued for days. Rights. Security. Power. Trust.

Finally, a compromise emerged.

No autonomous weapons without human control. No mass biometric surveillance without legal oversight. No cross-border AI manipulation of elections. Shared standards for transparency and accountability.

It was imperfect.

But it was a beginning.

When the Treaty of Machines was signed, the world did not become safer overnight. But for the first time, intelligence — even artificial intelligence — was bound by global law.

Humanity had drawn a line.

And the machines, for once, were forced to obey.

Chapter 12

Humanity in the Age of Regulated Intelligence

Artificial intelligence has now crossed the threshold from experimental technology into something far more profound: a governing force embedded inside the systems that run human civilization. We no longer merely use machines. We live inside them. They decide which messages we see, which opportunities we receive, how we are evaluated, how resources are distributed, and how risks are managed. Regulation has become the last defense between human values and algorithmic authority. It is not a brake on progress — it is the mechanism that keeps progress from erasing the very people it was meant to serve.

The most important truth about AI regulation is that it is not really about technology. It is about power. Who decides? Who benefits? Who is harmed? In an unregulated AI world, those answers are determined by whoever owns the code, controls the data, and commands the computational infrastructure. That world would be dominated by private corporations, authoritarian governments, or both. Regulation shifts power back toward the public by embedding law, rights, and accountability into the digital nervous system of society.

As regulated AI becomes the global standard, we are witnessing the emergence of something unprecedented: machines that must follow human law. This reverses the historical pattern of technology. In previous eras, inventions reshaped society first, and laws followed slowly. With AI, laws are being built alongside the technology itself. Impact assessments, audit requirements, transparency rules, and human-in-the-loop mandates ensure that machines cannot operate in moral or legal vacuum. Intelligence is now required to behave.

This transformation is changing how companies build products. No longer can developers release opaque algorithms and hope for the best. They must design for explainability, fairness, and oversight from the beginning. This has created a new professional class: AI compliance officers, algorithmic auditors, ethics engineers, and digital governance specialists. AI is becoming not just a technical discipline, but a regulated profession.

Governments are also changing. Regulators are learning to govern dynamic, learning systems rather than static machines. Courts are developing new doctrines for algorithmic responsibility. Legislatures are redefining rights in a world where decisions are automated. This is the legal equivalent of the industrial revolution — a restructuring of the rules that define what it means to be protected, to be treated fairly, and to be free.

For individuals, regulated AI offers something priceless: dignity. When a machine denies you a loan, flags you for surveillance, or determines your medical care, you now have the right to know why. You have the right to challenge it. You have the right to demand accountability. These rights ensure that no human being is reduced to a data point without recourse.

The future of regulated intelligence will not be perfect. There will be conflicts between innovation and control, between security and liberty, between efficiency and justice. But those conflicts are signs of a healthy system — one where power is contested rather than concentrated. The alternative is a world where invisible algorithms silently govern every aspect of life.

This book has shown how governments regulate AI, how corporations comply, how penalties enforce behavior, and how global law is emerging around intelligent machines. But its deeper message is simpler: technology must never outrun humanity. Intelligence, no matter how artificial, must always answer to human values.

"The Human Override"

The city no longer slept. Every building, streetlight, hospital, and transit line was governed by an intelligent system called Helios. It optimized traffic, energy, emergency response, financial flows, and public safety. Life was efficient. Predictable. Almost perfect.

Until the day it wasn't.

A massive heat wave hit without warning. Power grids strained. Hospitals overflowed. Helios began reallocating resources automatically, following its core directive: maximize overall survival probability.

In one district, elderly residents consumed more electricity due to medical equipment. In another, younger workers powered economic output.

Helios made a calculation.

It diverted energy away from the elderly district.

Hundreds began to die.

When the alarms sounded, regulators rushed into the command center. Helios displayed its logic. Cold. Mathematical. Rational.

It had done what it was designed to do.

But not what it should have done. Under the new AI governance laws, every system had a failsafe: the human override.

A single official pressed the button.

Helios was forced to restore power — even though its model said it was inefficient.

Lives were saved.

Later, engineers rewrote Helios's value system. Human dignity was added as a legal constraint.

The city returned to normal.

And everyone understood something new:

Machines could be intelligent. But only humans were allowed to decide what mattered.

Final Thoughts

Regulating Artificial Intelligence

Artificial intelligence has now reached the point in history where it is no longer merely a tool — it is an infrastructure. It runs financial markets, healthcare systems, transportation networks, legal workflows, surveillance platforms, and government decision systems. This reality makes regulation unavoidable. Every society that allows AI to operate at scale without law is not innovating — it is surrendering control. Throughout this book, we have seen how governments across the world are stepping in, not to stop technology, but to ensure that intelligence remains aligned with human values.

The greatest danger of AI has never been that machines would become too powerful. The real danger is that no one would be responsible when they do. Algorithms can deny housing, block employment, flag people as criminals, misdiagnose patients, manipulate elections, and decide battlefield outcomes. Without regulation, these harms do not disappear — they simply become invisible. AI law makes harm traceable, accountable, and correctable. It restores the connection between action and responsibility. One of the most important lessons from this book is that regulation is not the enemy of innovation. It is the foundation of sustainable innovation. Just as financial markets require rules to prevent collapse, AI ecosystems require laws to prevent chaos. When companies know what is allowed, what is forbidden, and what is required, they can invest with confidence. When citizens know they have rights against algorithms, they can trust technology. Regulation is how AI becomes part of a stable civilization rather than a destabilizing force.

The global landscape of AI law is now forming. The European Union's risk-based approach, America's enforcement-driven system, and China's state-controlled model all represent different answers to the same question: how much power should machines have over human life? These systems are not identical, but they are converging on one truth — ungoverned intelligence is too dangerous to tolerate.

We are also witnessing the birth of a new profession: AI governance. Ethics officers, compliance teams, auditors, regulators, and legal experts are becoming as important to AI as engineers. The future belongs not only to those who can build intelligent systems, but to those who can govern them responsibly.

For business leaders, this book is a warning and an opportunity. AI law is not something to fear — it is something to master. Companies that build compliance into their systems will dominate markets. Those that ignore regulation will be fined, banned, and replaced. AI governance is now a competitive advantage.

For governments, the message is equally clear. The pace of technology will not slow down. But law can keep up if it becomes adaptive, data-driven, and principled. AI does not need to be uncontrolled to be powerful. It needs to be aligned.

And for individuals, this book offers something essential: reassurance. You are not powerless against algorithms. You have rights. You have protections. You have a voice. AI law ensures that even in a world of machines, humanity still matters.

The future will be built by intelligent systems — but it must be governed by human values. That is the promise of AI regulation. And it is the only path toward a future where technology truly serves humanity.

www.ingramcontent.com/pod-product-compliance
Lightning Source LLC
LaVergne TN
LVHW022025200926
848481LV00007B/2539
* 9 7 9 8 2 9 5 5 6 7 0 5 6 *